POJ5-21

Having Fun with
PAINT

Sarah Medina

PowerKiDS
press.

New York

All projects should be done carefully, with an adult's help and supervision when appropriate (especially for activities involving cutting, carving, or sewing). An adult should execute or supervise any work with a craft knife, and safety scissiors should be used for all cutting.

Published in 2008 by The Rosen Publishing Group, Inc.
29 East 21st Street, New York, NY 10010

First Edition

Written by Sarah Medina
Produced by Calcium
Design and model making by Emma DeBanks
Photography by Tudor Photography
Consultancy and concepts by Lisa Regan

Library of Congress Cataloging-in-Publication Data

Medina, Sarah, 1960-
   Having fun with paint / Sarah Medina. -- 1st ed.
      p. cm. -- (Fun Art Projects)
      ISBN- 13: 978-1-4042-3718-6 (library binding)
      ISBN- 10: 1-4042-3718-6 (library binding)
      1. Handicraft--Juvenile literature. 2. Painting--Juvenile literature. I. Title.
   TT160.M3935 2007
      745.5--dc22
                                        2006027862

Manufactured in China

Contents

Fun with Paint!

There are lots of different types of paint, such as poster paints and oil paints. People usually paint with a paintbrush, but you can also paint using a toothbrush, or by dipping paper into paint that has been mixed with water. These are some of the things you will need to make the projects in this book:

- Poster board
- Food coloring
- Oil paints
- Paper
- Poster paints

- Fresh fruit (grapes, a banana, and an orange)

Note for adults
Children may need adult assistance with some of the project steps. Turn to page 23 for Further Ideas.

Read the "You will need" boxes carefully for
a full list of what you need to make each project.

Things to remember!

• Find a surface where you can make the projects.

• Find an apron to cover your clothes, or
some old clothes that can get messy.

• Ask an adult to help with cutting or other
things that might be tricky to do on your own.

Funky Flowerpot

Make a funky flowerpot for a pretty plant!

1 Stick reinforcement rings and strips of masking tape in lines around your plant pot.

2 Dip your toothbrush in paint, and dab around parts of the plant pot.

3 Repeat using different colors, until the plant pot is covered with paint.

4 When the paint is dry, peel off the reinforcement rings and strips of masking tape.

5 Put a pretty plant into your plant pot!

Magical Butterfly

Create a magical picture to put on your wall!

You will need
- 1 large sheet of paper
- Sequins
- Paintbrush
- Poster paints
- Glue

1 Fold a piece of paper in half and open it up again.

2 On one half of the paper, paint the outline of half a butterfly, up to the fold in the paper.

4 Before the paint dries, fold the paper back in half and press down on it firmly. Open it up and allow to dry.

3 Paint the butterfly's wing with a thick layer of paint. You can use more than one color if you want to!

5 Glue sequins on the butterfly's antennae.

Gift Wrap

Make a present extra-special with your own wrapping paper design.

You will need
- 1 large sheet of paper
- Food coloring
- Plastic spoon
- Paintbrush
- Water

1 Brush clean water all over the paper.

2 While the paper is still wet, use a spoon to drop food coloring on the paper.

4 Watch the color spread all over the paper!

5 Allow it to dry. Use your wrapping paper to wrap a gift!

3 While the food coloring is still wet, blow gently on the colors in different directions.

Still Life with Fruit

Surprise your family and friends with this modern art project!

You will need
- Small bunch of grapes
- Banana
- Orange
- 1 sheet of paper
- Paintbrush
- Pencil
- Poster paints—blue, red, and purple

color wheel

1 Lay your fruit on the table in front of you, and look at the color wheel. Notice the colors on the wheel that are on the opposite side of the colors of the fruit.

3 Paint the banana in its opposite color on the color wheel.

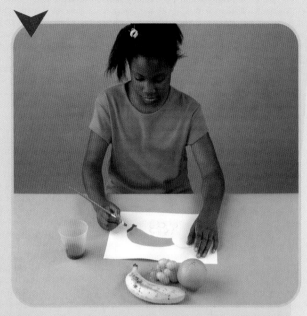

2 Draw a picture of the fruit on the paper.

4 Paint the orange in its opposite color.

5 Paint the grapes in their opposite color.

Marbled Gift Tags

People will love these marbled gift tags!

You will need

- Foil tray
- 2 tubes of oil paint—
  1 light color and
  1 dark color
- Ribbon
- Plastic spoon
- 1 sheet of
  poster board
- Hole punch
- Paper towel
- Scissors
- Water

1 Put some water in the tray, so it is two fingers deep. Gently swirl in a spoonful of each paint color.

2 Cut the poster board into four pieces.

3 Place a piece of poster board on the top of the water, and gently move it around.

4 Remove the poster board carefully, and allow to dry on paper towel. The painted side should face upward. Repeat steps 3 and 4.

5 Fold each piece of poster board in half, make a hole on one side, and tie a piece of ribbon through the hole.

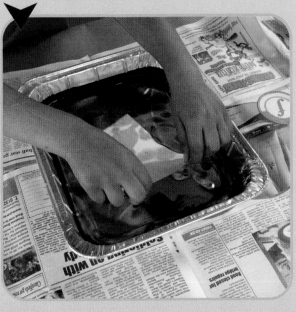

 Ask an adult for help with cutting poster board!

Flowerpot Person

Cheer up a plant with this flowerpot person!

You will need
- Large wooden spoon
- 1 sheet of white poster board
- Paintbrush
- Pencil
- Poster paints including yellow and green
- Glue
- Scissors

1 Place the spoon on the poster board. Draw large petals around the top of the spoon.

2 Cut the petals out, then paint them in one color or in different colors.

3 Paint the spoon handle green, and then paint the spoon face yellow.

5 Glue the petals onto the back of the spoon face!

4 Paint a mouth, nose, and two eyes on the spoon face.

 Ask an adult for help with cutting poster board!

Door Hanger

Make a door hanger with a night sky for bedtime and a shining sun for morning!

You will need
- I white wax candle
- I sheet of thick white poster board
- I 12-in. (30-cm) piece of ribbon
- Hole punch
- Paintbrush
- Poster paints—black and orange

1 Using the wax candle, draw a moon and planets on one side of the poster board.

2 Paint it black and watch the picture appear! Allow to dry.

4 Punch two holes in the corners of the poster board, and tie a ribbon on it.

3 On the other side, use the candle to draw a large sun and its rays. Paint the poster board orange and allow to dry.

5 Hang on your bedroom door.

 Ask an adult to help punch holes in the poster board!

Camouflaged Toy Box

Make a secret place to store your toys!

You will need

- 1 large box with a lid
- 2 large pieces of cardboard
- Paintbrush
- Poster paints— green and light brown
- Scissors

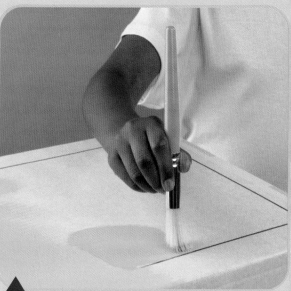

1 Paint the box and lid with light brown paint, and allow to dry.

2 Paint camouflage patterns on the box and lid with green paint.

3 Ask an adult to cut one piece of cardboard so that it is the same height, but slightly less wide than the long side of the box.

4 Ask an adult to cut the second piece of cardboard so that it is the same height, but less wide than the short side of the box.

5 Ask an adult to cut a straight line down the middle of each of the two pieces of cardboard. Do not cut all the way to the end!

6 Slide the longer piece of cardboard into the middle of the box.

7 Slide the smaller piece of cardboard into the box to make four separate sections for your toys.

 Ask an adult for help with cutting cardboard!

22

Further Ideas

Here are some exciting finishing touches you can add to your projects.

Funky Flowerpot

Paint a big, bright flower on the front of the plant pot!

Magical Butterfly

Glue sequins all over the butterfly's wings to make them shine!

Gift Wrap

Use colorful pens to write your own messages, such as HAPPY BIRTHDAY, on the paper.

Still Life with Fruit

Add some other fruits, such as cherries, to the still life, using the opposite colors on the color wheel.

Marbled Gift Tags

Dab glue on the gift tags, sprinkle some glitter onto the glue, and then shake off the excess glitter.

Flowerpot Person

Glue wobbly eyes onto the flowerpot man, or instead, glue on buttons for the eyes!

Door Hanger

Stick shiny gold and silver stars on the door hanger for added sparkle!

Camouflaged Toy Box (Ask an adult for help with making holes.)

Use pieces of string to make handles for your chest. Carefully press two holes in each side of the box, thread the string through, and tie a knot inside to keep it in place.

Glossary

camouflage a disguise using the same colors as the background, so the camouflaged item blends in

color wheel all the main colors arranged in a circle, to show which colors look best together

marbling with a swirly pattern that looks like the naturally occurring pattern in marble (a kind of stone)

masking tape tape that is not very sticky, so it peels off easily

oil paint paint made with oil and color, which is very sticky and takes a long time to dry

poster paint paint made with a kind of glue that dries quickly and gives bright colors

still life a picture of an arrangement of objects (instead of a portrait or landscape)

Index

Web Sites

Due to the changing nature of internet links, Powerkids Press has developed an online list of Web sites related to the subject of this book. This site is updated regularly. Please use this link to access the list:
www.powerkidslinks.com/ldo/paint/